Samuel French Acting Edition

Mud Row

by Dominique Morisseau

D1519522

‖SAMUEL FRENCH‖

ISBN 978-0-573-70859-6

www.concordtheatricals.com
www.concordtheatricals.co.uk

FOR PRODUCTION INQUIRIES

UNITED STATES AND CANADA
info@concordtheatricals.com
1-866-979-0447

UNITED KINGDOM AND EUROPE
licensing@concordtheatricals.co.uk
020-7054-7200

Each title is subject to availability from Concord Theatricals Corp.,
depending upon country of performance. Please be aware that *MUD
ROW* may not be licensed by Concord Theatricals Corp. in your
territory. Professional and amateur producers should contact the
nearest Concord Theatricals Corp. office or licensing partner to verify
availability.

This work is published by Samuel French, an imprint of Concord
Theatricals Corp.

MUD ROW was first produced by People's Light (Abigail Adams, Executive Artistic Director; Zak Berkman, Producing Director) in Malvern, Pennsylvania on June 26, 2019. The performance was directed by Steve H. Broadnax III, with sets by Michael Carnahan, costumes by Shilla Benning, lights by Kathy Perkins, sound by Curtis Craig, and dramaturgy by Gina Pisale. The production stage manager was Kate McSorley. The cast was as follows:

ELSIE	Tiffany Rachelle Stewart
FRANCES	Gillian Glasco
REGINE	Nikkole Salter
TOSHI	Renika Williams
DAVIN	Bjorn DuPaty
TYRIEK	Eric Robinson, Jr.

MUD ROW was a 2018 recipient of an Edgerton Foundation New Play Award.

CHARACTERS

ELSIE – (20s, can be played by women in their 40s to give the appearance of age and time) Black Woman. Poised. Proper. Soft. Desperate to find a sense of belonging.

FRANCES – (20s, can be played by women in their 40s to give the appearance of age and time) Black Woman. Tough. Fighter. Persistent. Not easily contained, especially when she believes in something.

REGINE – (25-40) Black Woman. Well-educated. Reserved. Guarded and worrisome. Wife to Davin. Sister to Toshi. Somewhere a vulnerable and fragile soul.

TOSHI – (25-28) Black Woman. Fiesty. Impulsive. Resistant. Rough around the edges and a former drug addict. Girlfriend to Tyriek. Sister to Regine. Somewhere a deep and wise soul.

DAVIN – (35-40) Black Man. Patient. Supportive. Optimistic. Can be pushy in his positivity. Husband to Regine.

TYRIEK – (28-30) Black Man. Sharp. Calculating. Former thug looking for a second chance at life. Boyfriend to Toshi.

ACT I

Prologue

(A glimpse of the past: sepia tone.)

(In silhouette, a woman, **ELSIE** *stands posed as if in a picture.)*

(Lights up and she comes fully to life, as if stepping out of the moment in the picture into full reality.)

(She stands before a mirror in a slip and handling pearls. She dolls herself up.)

ELSIE. They was all two, three story houses. All had different names. There was Thumblatch Row. No idea what that meant. Academy Row. Those is the houses built on the side of old West Chester Academy. Mechanics Row. You can guess who lived there. Bunch of mechanics all together. That's a whole different kinda segregation. Job segregation, I guess. But some people wouldn't call it segregation. Just living around people they got somethin' in common with. It's a funny thing to try to name somethin' people just do on their natural. Like maybe if mechanics like each other that much they oughta have a row together. There was Peanut Row – them was for the smaller houses right over there by Walnut Street. I thought, naturally, maybe they ate lots of peanuts. But that wasn't it. It was built by dried fruit dealers. But who cares about dried fruit dealers. And in that case, why didn't they name it Dried Fruit Row? There was Bread Row, built near Poplar and

Market Streets by a confectioner and bread baker. That makes sense. Cabbage Row but that didn't have nothin' to do with cabbage. And then of course it was towns. Riggtown. Willistown. And Georgetown. That was the Colored area. Named after some guy – George somebody. Or somebody George. Anyway, the Colored area is east of the railroad tracks. By Goose Creek. Where all the sewage from the town flows. One of the filthiest creeks to flow near West Chester. And that's where they called it. Some say Mud Row was a different part of town, not here. But it makes sense, I think. That Coloreds bein' the mud of the world...livin' in mud-like conditions...would naturally be in Mud Row. I don't know the answers. I'm just learnin' cuz we got to know how we got somewhere, so we know how to get somewhere else. Nobody wanna be stuck in the mud. Not nobody.

(*She finishes the last touches on her hair.*)

Whatcha think Fran?

(*Lights up on* **FRANCES**. *As if she, too, is stepping from the photograph at the call of her name.*)

FRANCES. Not too much lipstick. Don't want to be Jezebel. Just Billie Holiday or somethin'. This fella is sort of upstanding, ain't he?

ELSIE. He's studying History and Education at Cheney Training School for Teachers.

FRANCES. Thas why you quoting Row this and fact that, you tryin' to impress your date?

ELSIE. I'm trying to learn so we know how we got somewhere –

FRANCES. You said that already, Lawd! I'm 'bout two quotes away from chokin' you.

ELSIE. Don't be simple.

FRANCES. Don't call me simple.

ELSIE. And don't be contrary.

FRANCES. I ain't contrary.

ELSIE. He's opening up a world for me. I won't be the same.

FRANCES. Just don't be too different, or I swear Elsie... If you start soundin' like any of these highfalutin Coloreds I might have to disown you.

ELSIE. You could study with me.

FRANCES. Or I could not and still be fine.

ELSIE. Frances –

FRANCES. Here, let's make sure you tightened those pearls good.

> (**FRANCES** *fastens* **ELSIE***'s pearls. Looks at her one good time.*)

There, you look high society. Nobody would ever know.

ELSIE. Know what?

FRANCES. That you was born of a whore mama and an indecent daddy.

ELSIE. Don't say that.

FRANCES. Go. Blend with the highfalutin Coloreds. But you 'member somethin' sister dearest.

ELSIE. What's that?

FRANCES. At the core of who we always been...is love and fight and togetherness. No matter what new worlds you see, as long as you keep that in you through to the soul, you gonna be a special woman.

> (**ELSIE** *hugs* **FRANCES**, *filled with emotion.*)

> (*As lights fade on these sisters, a flash happens!*)

> (*They are frozen in photograph – forever hugging.*)

Scene One

(Present day: blueish green.)

(Lights up on an abandoned home. Some things lain around, old and dusty. Something like a painting from 1979. An old rug. A B&W television in a corner.)

(REGINE *and* **DAVIN** *enter the dark space.)*

REGINE. It's been years.

DAVIN. Watch your steps baby. It's really dark.

REGINE. The smell is unfamiliar.

DAVIN. Maybe there's a light switch?

> *(He feels up against the wall. Flicks the light. Nothing.)*

REGINE. Oh shit. Did we forget light bulbs?

DAVIN. Gotta be some here.

REGINE. Five years empty. You think?

DAVIN. I'll go look.

REGINE. I'll go with you.

DAVIN. No baby. Too dangerous. Let me.

> **(DAVIN** *turns on his phone light. It makes a loud hissing sound before activating.)*

REGINE. Jesus, the sound of that thing! Can't you figure out how to silence that?

DAVIN. It's the sound the app makes.

REGINE. Davin, if there are squatters or addicts hiding out, they're gonna hear us coming.

DAVIN. Why would there be addicts –

REGINE. I'm just saying – IF.

DAVIN. Baby don't start. Nobody's here.

REGINE. These places have squatters. I've read about it.

DAVIN. Regine, we just got here. Let's not start with the paranoia until day two, okay? I'm gonna go find us some light bulbs.

REGINE. Be careful.

DAVIN. Yep.

> (**DAVIN** *disappears into the next room.* **REGINE**
> *stands cautiously against the door. The*
> *moonlight is her only source.)*

REGINE. *(Offstage.)* How completely stupid was I to attempt
this at night?

DAVIN. *(Offstage.)* It gets dark early. We had to come
eventually.

REGINE. *(Offstage.)* This was premature. This isn't fully
thinking. I'm not fully thinking.

> *(Silence.)*

> (**REGINE** *takes baby steps around the living*
> *room. She touches an old plastic covering*
> *over a couch.)*

(In disbelief / to herself.) Place is empty for five years
and the plastic is still on the couch. That woman…

> *(A noise of things falling. Probably cans.)*

DAVIN. *(Offstage.)* Ahhh / shit!

REGINE. Davin???? What was that, you alright?

DAVIN. *(Offstage.)* Just stay out there. Don't come in here.

REGINE. What was that?

DAVIN. *(Offstage.)* Some old can full of – is this grease?!

REGINE. What kind of grease?

DAVIN. *(Offstage.)* Cooking grease! Gotdamnit!

REGINE. Baby, we're gonna make a mess. Let's just leave.

DAVIN. *(Offstage.)* Found it!

> (**DAVIN** *walks back in the room. Cooking*
> *grease over his arms and shirt. He's a mess.*
> *But a triumphant mess. In his hands, a pack*
> *of light bulbs.)*

> (**REGINE** *sits on the plastic covered couch.)*

Let's see if these babies work.

(He heads to a lamp.)

REGINE. Ugh, baby. You smell.

DAVIN. Cooking grease in an old coffee can. If that ain't a sign of grandma's house, I don't know what is.

REGINE. You can take a shower as soon as we get back to the hotel.

*(**DAVIN** flicks on a lamp. Success!)*

(The walls are a dingy blueish green. Wallpaper is peeling. Water stains from a leak. This was once a very nice house. There is the suggestion underneath some ruin.)

DAVIN. Huh.

REGINE. This is...

DAVIN. Yours.

REGINE. This is not mine.

DAVIN. It is for now.

REGINE. It doesn't look like I remember.

DAVIN. Five years isn't that long ago baby.

REGINE. That's how long she's been gone. But I haven't been here since...

   ...

   ...

   a teen.

DAVIN. That long? Really? You didn't tell me that.

REGINE. It wasn't worth talking about much.

DAVIN. How'd you measure that?

REGINE. Memories can be oppressive.

DAVIN. So this is your first time ba / ck –

REGINE. Think we can get more light?

DAVIN. We'll see how far this eight-pack gets us when we walk through.

REGINE. I don't want to walk through. I feel weird. Like I'm moving backwards...

DAVIN. You're trippin' baby. It's not that bad. Check it – is that a black and white TV?

REGINE. Unreal.

(**DAVIN** *goes over to it. He plugs it in. Nothing.*)

DAVIN. We gotta get this to work. Collector's item. Could sell it to a museum.

REGINE. We actually used to watch that. When we were like three or four or something. Me and my...

(She stops.)

DAVIN. Your sister.

(Pause.)

(**REGINE** *stiffens at the thought. Doesn't wish to go there. Moves around the room. The floor creaks. She steps on the creak spots to confirm – yep, creaky.)*

REGINE. The appraiser is coming at what time?

DAVIN. Four o'clock tomorrow.

REGINE. I can't imagine more than a hundred thousand.

DAVIN. Some houses over here are going for two forty. I looked it up.

REGINE. These walls. Old floors. Amount of work needed in this living room alone. May make more sense to knock the house down and build another one.

DAVIN. I don't know how you can say that with such detachment.

REGINE. I am detached.

DAVIN. Not in blood and legacy. You still have shreds of yourself here. Don't undermine that.

REGINE. This place doesn't even smell familiar.

DAVIN. It's been awhile.

REGINE. Sense memory. Something is supposed to be tugging at my nostalgia right now. But all I feel is cold and distance. I'm ready to go, Davin. We can come back in the morning when it's more sunlight.

DAVIN. We should do a walk-through, at least. So we can see what we're looking at before the appraisers try to determine the value for us.

REGINE. Two weeks ago I didn't even know this house was mine. Now all of a sudden some developer guy takes interest and I find out the deed's been in my name since childhood. And no one cared to tell me.

DAVIN. They were investing in your future.

REGINE. Meanwhile neglecting me in my present. And now I'm supposed to be invested in it?

DAVIN. Gotta decide our own value before folks start placing price tags on us.

REGINE. I know you think this is a gift, but it's the house of my teenage angst. Lot of baggage here. I can feel the ghosts creeping back in and I don't make any room for them.

DAVIN. Then let's go. We'll come back in the morning. That better?

REGINE. Maybe.

(**DAVIN** *grabs* **REGINE** *by the hand. He pulls her close to him.*)

DAVIN. In a couple of days, this place is going to completely disappear from your grasp. You won't be able to turn over a rug or peel back wallpaper to confront whatever the hell you're running from. You've closed off this part of yourself from me. Maybe this is your chance to get free. You get me baby? You've been running from this place a long time. But you can't run forever.

(*She grabs his face.*)

REGINE. Maybe just a little while longer.

(*They kiss.* **REGINE** *grabs* **DAVIN**'s *hand and pulls him out of the house.*)

(*They left the light on.*)

Scene Two

(Present day: magenta.)

(TOSHI *opens the door to the house. It is now much later at night.)*

TOSHI. See this shit?!?!? Somebody's been up in our shit!

(TOSHI *looks behind her and sees no one. She goes back to the door.)*

Tyriek are you for real? You gonna just stay out here?

TYRIEK. I was comin'. You actin' all emergency. You movin' too fast.

TOSHI. Cuz somebody's been up in our shit!

TYRIEK. And if they were still here…what was you gonna do, exactly? Hunh?

TOSHI. Kick their asses out.

TYRIEK. On what grounds?

TOSHI. Possession. We've been occupying this space for…

TYRIEK. 'Bout three months.

TOSHI. It's our home then. Legal.

TYRIEK. Toshi you know ain't nothin' 'bout our whole operation legal.

TOSHI. Don't say that.

TYRIEK. I'm sayin' it. Truth hurts.

TOSHI. I told you I saw somebody snoopin' 'round here the other day. But you don't listen to me. You never listen.

TYRIEK. That's cuz you talk A LOT. I gotta be selective 'bout how much of you I let bleed through.

TOSHI. Tyriek. I am not going to fight with you. *(Quick shift.)* Look at this. They found our light bulb stash. Who told them they can use our stuff like it's theirs?

TYRIEK. Not exactly ours.

TOSHI. *(Ignoring him.)* Like they can just come up in here and lay hand and foot wherever they please.

TYRIEK. At least they put the bulbs in the actual lamps. You be on some conservation shit that is impossible.

TOSHI. When you steal electricity, you have to be selective fool. Can't have it in every room. House gets plenty of sunlight. But obviously whoever was up in here is all privileged and what not. Don't have to conserve. Can just be liberal and waste our – oh shit wait!

TYRIEK. *(Sharing the epiphany.)* How'd they get the electricity in here????

TOSHI. Did they move our wires? How in the hell????

> (**TOSHI** *walks into the kitchen. From offstage, we hear her.*)

(Offstage.) They spilled our grease?!?!?! Bastards!!!!

> (*A light comes from the kitchen.* **TOSHI** *re-enters.*)

T, they got electricity.

TYRIEK. How'd they do that?

TOSHI. This is not good. This is not good at all.

TYRIEK. Like official electricity?

TOSHI. This is crazy. This ain't streets. This is somebody proper.

TYRIEK. So wait though. You think somebody's got papers?

TOSHI. In five years, who just come up out the blue layin' claim over here?

TYRIEK. Maybe some family –

TOSHI. Don't say nothin' to me about family. Ain't been no family around here. All these touches of care, ancient brittle hands is what molded it. And that old woman gone now and ain't nobody lay claim here since. This is our space. We embraced it like it's our inheritance. All the work she likely put in over the years, we pickin' up that work and keepin' it goin'. That's worth rent money and then some. So it's ours. And that's what I'll tell anybody try to evict us.

TYRIEK. You also gon' tell 'em what we do for a living?

TOSHI. What we DID for a living.

TYRIEK. Same difference.

TOSHI. I will not be assigned the shame of my former sins eternally. Since we've been here we've been straight and flyin' right. I do not exist beyond three months ago. That Toshi is dead.

TYRIEK. That was the Toshi I fell in love with.

TOSHI. That Tyriek is also dead. If he don't know it, I'll gladly kill him again just to be sure.

TYRIEK. You kill me and you won't have nobody to bitch at.

TOSHI. I'll bitch at the brick walls or the wood floors. Talkin' to you is just the same sometimes anyway.

TYRIEK. Should we check out the rest of the house? See what they been up to? They mighta taken some more of our stuff.

TOSHI. I need to sit down. I'm getting premonitions.

TYRIEK. Right now? Right now you gettin' premonitions?

TOSHI. Yes. Sit next to me.

TYRIEK. Toshi I don't know how this is gonna –

TOSHI. Sit. Down.

(**TYRIEK** *sits next to* **TOSHI** *reluctantly.*)

I'm seeing colors.

TYRIEK. *(Unenthused.)* Colors.

TOSHI. Magentas. Lots of magentas.

TYRIEK. Uh hunh.

TOSHI. I don't know what magenta means. You know what it means?

TYRIEK. I don't know baby. The book is...upstairs or somewhere...

TOSHI. I think magenta is the color of anxiety. Or no, depression. Or wait...

TYRIEK. This doesn't seem productive –

TOSHI. Oh no, it's not that. Those are the negative effects. It's the color of balance. Yes, or harmony. I think harmony.

TYRIEK. OK, great. Clock that. We'll figure out the purpose of it before we die.

TOSHI. Tyriek. I'm being serious.

TYRIEK. OK, then. What you wanna do? You seein' the color of harmony and so... What's that got to do with somebody movin' through our shit?

TOSHI. Everything has a purpose. Something is coming into this space. Something magenta. I feel strange.

TYRIEK. Don't freak out. I got you.

TOSHI. You got me? Two seconds ago the light from outside had you too shook to enter this place. Now I'm supposed to breathe deep cuz you got me?

TYRIEK. You doubtin' my role as protector now?

TOSHI. I'm doubtin' your focus.

TYRIEK. You don't need to doubt me Toshi. I'm not the one who's renegade and occupying territories like I have some right to other people's spaces just cuz I say so. I ride with you on this cuz it means somethin' to you. That's good enough for me. But if our ride is up, we may have to take that and go somewhere else. That's just the way the mud flows when you livin' life vagabond-style.

TOSHI. I'm sick of livin' life vagabond-style.

TYRIEK. We don't have to. We can scrounge these pennies together and get in on that public housing –

TOSHI. I'm not doing public housing again.

TYRIEK. What's wrong with public housing? I grew up in public housing.

TOSHI. I didn't say anything was wrong with it.

TYRIEK. You bein' elitist while squattin'?

TOSHI. I'm not bein' elitist. Don't call me that. I am not the sins of my foremothers.

TYRIEK. We not talkin' your foremothers or grandmothers or mother's mother's mothers. We talkin' about this you and your attitude that needs more renovation than this house. You thinkin' the wrong way.

TOSHI. Tyriek, nobody made aware of our questionable past is going to approve us for any type of housing loan. We have been boxed out of the social circle of trust. There is no redemption in this cruel world.

TYRIEK. I thought we weren't going to carry the sins of our past.

TOSHI. We don't have to carry them. Society will carry it for us. We'll never be clean in their eyes. Don't you get that? We are the outcast. The black sheep. I've always been the black sheep. In my family. In my community. In this entire gray world when I'm tryin' to be magenta.

TYRIEK. We back to magenta now.

TOSHI. I'm speaking in metaphor. Can you comprehend?

TYRIEK. What I comprehend is you in denial, baby.

TOSHI. Here we go with the / psycho-analyzation.

TYRIEK. About your part in this reckless livin' we have found ourselves in. And in all our precariousness –

TOSHI. Million dollar words / now.

TYRIEK. We can't overlook that not more than half a year ago we were still engaging in the trade of stealing credit card numbers and running e-mail scams to bleed America's privileged dry without so much as a small twinge of remorse –

TOSHI. There was some / remorse.

TYRIEK. In an effort to support our not so elegant drug habits.

TOSHI. I was depressed. That was a clinical diagnosis. Not paranoia.

TYRIEK. Doesn't matter baby. Bankers and Real Estate Agents are not going to care about your reasons and clinical diagnoses.

They're not going to care about you popping pills for your uncontrollable depression and getting hooked to the narcotics instead of confronting your demons. They're going to say – Toshi Geter, DENIED.

TOSHI. I already know that.

TYRIEK. Toshi Geter, DENIAL.

TOSHI. Stop Tyriek.

TYRIEK. Toshi Geter, Take Some Responsibility –

TOSHI. SHUT UP TYRIEK!

    (Beat.)

TYRIEK. I'm not trying to be an asshole.

TOSHI. Too bad. You're quite a natural.

TYRIEK. I love you Toshi. As hateful as you can make loving you, I still do it.

TOSHI. And I still love you. It's the only reason I haven't killed you in your sleep.

TYRIEK. But if we are going to atone for the sins of our past...if we are truly kicking this lifestyle and moving onto something better, we have to let go. We have to be willing to take an L and just move on.

TOSHI. What makes you think we have to move on?

TYRIEK. Tosh, whoever is snoopin' around this place ain't gonna to stop 'til they get whatever they looking for. They got electricity. They're all up in this piece. They must want it for somethin'. I don't think we should wait around to see what for.

TOSHI. The least I'm going to do is wait around to see what for.

TYRIEK. Toshi –

TOSHI. I'm owed that, Tyriek. AT LEAST. This isn't just an empty cardboard box we found. For three months we've been here without anybody asking questions. Maybe they decided they better not. Maybe they're just minding their own business. Or maybe they know we need somewhere to be and they aren't turning us over to the streets. Maybe next door to the right and the left is some shred of humanity. Some people that don't see us as our former selves, don't believe we're criminals or scum, don't think of us as a threat. Maybe they know that if we weren't here, we'd be nowhere.

TYRIEK. You think the people over here givin' you that much of the benefit of doubt?

TOSHI. I do.

TYRIEK. Why would they do that Tosh? What sense would that make?

TOSHI. The heart don't gotta make logic sense. The heart makes incomprehensible sense.

TYRIEK. Maybe they just waitin' for the day when the po-pos come and haul us outta here.

TOSHI. Nah. They know me. I think they know me.

TYRIEK. As in remember you?

TOSHI. Maybe.

TYRIEK. That ain't gonna mean nothin' if some developer or realtor is comin' to lay claim.

TOSHI. Maybe we can stop them from layin' claim. Or scare them off. At least for awhile.

TYRIEK. Scare them off.

TOSHI. You down?

TYRIEK. You got a plan?

TOSHI. We can build one.

TYRIEK. Am I gonna lose you if I'm not down?

TOSHI. You already know.

TYRIEK. I need time to weigh my options.

TOSHI. We need to do some investigating. Snoop on the snoopers. Find out whassup before we go wavin' white flags. Legit or not, we know this place better than anybody.

TYRIEK. Baby, you got a determined troubled mind and I find that shit very sexy in this moment.

TOSHI. Light a candle.

(*TYRIEK finds a nearby candle and obeys.*)

Let's bless every room in this house so it remembers who it truly belongs to.

(**TOSHI** *grabs* **TYRIEK** *and kisses him passionately. Lights shift.*)

Scene Three

> *(Sepia tone:* **FRANCES** *and* **ELSIE** *in a new framed position.* **FRANCES** *steps out of the moment. She is making protest signs.)*

> *(***ELSIE*** *steps out and begins brushing her hair in the mirror.)*

ELSIE. All along these grounds, right where Ms. Esther's house is and Mr. Pickney's used to be, there was this safe haven of houses for the runaway slaves. Call it the Underground Railroad. And all the Quakers what used to be over here was participants, puttin' up they house to shelter those runaways and hide them from the law. And Edmund says –

FRANCES. Edmund / says.

ELSIE. – that we are all living over the shadows of those slaves. Those former slaves turned free men and women, turned Quakers, who believed in bein' a friend to anyone in need of social, moral, or physical help. Edmund says we have a responsibility as new Colored folk /

FRANCES. New Colored / folk.

ELSIE. – who have been afforded opportunities that our foremothers and fathers were not.

FRANCES. Who is these new Colored folk? And what happens to the old Colored folk? Where they 'spose to go?

ELSIE. Oh Frances it isn't literal.

FRANCES. I be damned if it ain't.

ELSIE. You have to give him a chance. You have to give him a real chance. You'll see he's just a brilliant man who's gonna find his place in the highest parts of society.

FRANCES. That's all you give two shits about.

ELSIE. It isn't.

FRANCES. Belonging to high society ain't all to it. You got to have yo' eye on the folk who ain't so lucky to get their education and papers and such.

ELSIE. There is a talented tenth who must move us beyond the ranks of second class –

FRANCES. Don't tell me nothin' 'bout yo' talented tenth.

ELSIE. It isn't mine. It's the intellectual W.E.B DuBois, and Edmund –

FRANCES. Elsie you done already quoted talented tenth to me several million times. I know what it sayin'.

ELSIE. Why must you speak so savagely about it?

FRANCES. Ain't speakin' savagely. I just don't like that kinda talk. It sound siddity.

ELSIE. What's wrong with bein' of class and stature?

FRANCES. What's wrong with not bein' of it?

ELSIE. Oh God. You're just contrary for the sake of contrary.

FRANCES. Listen to what this fella got you thinkin' like. Like it's somethin' wrong with what you already come from. He know your roots? He know your upbringing?

ELSIE. He doesn't say it's anything wrong with it.

FRANCES. Does he know it?

ELSIE. We haven't gotten to that part yet.

FRANCES. Ain't you? Sound like you done got way past that part by my speculations.

ELSIE. What you want, Frances? You want me to stop seein' him?

FRANCES. I want you to stop quotin' him.

ELSIE. I like to quote him.

FRANCES. Pass me that glue.

> (**ELSIE** *passes* **FRANCES** *glue.* **FRANCES** *takes the glue and begins to gluing a stick to a sign.)*

> (**ELSIE** *looks at* **FRANCES** *for a moment.)*

ELSIE. That smells somethin' awful.

FRANCES. Open a window or shut your mouth.

ELSIE. Must you do this?

FRANCES. Why wouldn't I?

ELSIE. The way to change society is through education, Frances. Through becoming a person of greatness against all odds.

FRANCES. The way to change society is to stand with this sign outside Jerry's Lunch Shop and demand they serve Coloreds or else take a brick through a window.

ELSIE. Frances! You won't do that.

FRANCES. Who say I ain't?

ELSIE. What good is this sign going to do?

FRANCES. Speak louder than our voices can carry.

ELSIE. You and all those other folk down there... You're going to get yourself hurt. Nobody is going to change this way. Nobody is going to start all of a sudden serving Coloreds because they read your sign.

FRANCES. The sign ain't to make the people doin' the dirt change. The sign is for all them folk on the fence. We go stand down there disgruntled, and I betcha some folk who wuz just livin' White, ignant and passive will start thinkin' different 'bout theyselves. Wonderin' what kinda fool they is to not even wanna share a counter with other living beings. The sign sinks in a message to 'em. Maybe they ought not eat at this Lunch Shop 'til we can too.

ELSIE. Well that's silly.

FRANCES. No sillier than you quotin' talented tenths and highfalutin gentlemen friends.

ELSIE. Don't call him that.

FRANCES. You got your ways of makin' things better. I got mine.

ELSIE. Where you meetin' these folk?

FRANCES. Gonna gather over at the Community Center and march on down Gay Street.

ELSIE. Don't get yourself hurt.

FRANCES. Don't get yo'self hurt neither.

> (**FRANCES** *gathers her sign. Holds it up high.*
> *It reads:*)

("*WHITES-ONLY SERVE ALL.*")

How's it look?

ELSIE. It could stand to be a bit more poetic.

FRANCES. You be poetic. I'll be to the point.

ELSIE. I really wish you would give Edmund a chance.

FRANCES. Tell him to come on down to stand with us at Jerry's Lunch Shop and I'll give him all the chances he can take.

ELSIE. Frances. I'm pregnant.

> (*Beat.* **FRANCES** *sets down her sign. Looks blankly at her sister.*)

FRANCES. He know?

ELSIE. Not yet.

FRANCES. He don't know your past. He don't know your present. But you thinkin' of makin' him part of your future?

ELSIE. I love him.

FRANCES. You can't select the parts of you for somebody to love. They gots to love you whole.

ELSIE. I'll tell him when the time is right.

FRANCES. That time better be real soon.

ELSIE. Frances I'm afraid.

> (**FRANCES** *moves to her sister. She grabs her by the hands.*)

FRANCES. You ain't got nothin' to be afraid of. It been rougher than this. We got us a house what used to be part of that railroad you was talkin' 'bout. We comin' out the shadows of the slaves and those free men and women who was tryin' to make somethin' of theyselves on they own. We come from a mama who whored, true. But she left us a house to keep for ourselves. And we come from a daddy who run off, but he gave us his last name. That count for somethin'. That make us Geters. And we strong and full of ways to last. You ain't got nothin' to be afraid of. All you got to do is 'member who you are.

*(***FRANCES*** touches **ELSIE***'s chin.)*

(Flash.)

(They are immortalized.)

Scene Four

(Present day: red.)

(Daylight spills through the windows of the living room of the old house.)

*(**REGINE** moves the couch around. **DAVIN** comes down the stairs, reluctant to tell her something.)*

REGINE. How's the upstairs?

DAVIN. It's um...it's pretty spacious. Got four bedrooms up there, but one of 'em was turned into a sewing room. Looks um...looks old...

REGINE. *(Preoccupied.)* Something about this room feels slightly different.

DAVIN. Now that we're seeing this place in the daylight, I gotta tell you baby –

REGINE. It has a new smell to it. Like someone's been burning candles.

DAVIN. I think somebody's living here.

REGINE. What?

DAVIN. Yeah. Looks like it. But don't panic. Let's just take it slow and figure this out in calm.

REGINE. You think they were here last night?

DAVIN. Had to be. There's a used toothbrush in the upstairs bathroom.

REGINE. Oh God! That's horrible!

DAVIN. Might be someone homeless, baby.

REGINE. That's not good Davin! We're going to have to evict them. Fuck! You can't just go live in someone else's house. Don't they know that you can't do that?

DAVIN. It's getting cold out. Maybe this is all they have.

REGINE. What if they're addicts or... I mean, this could get dangerous. I don't think we should be here without the police, Davin. I think we should call the police.

DAVIN. Maybe you're right.

REGINE. In my grandmother's house. There are strangers living in my grandmother's house.

DAVIN. We should wait for the appraiser to get here. It's just another thirty minutes.

REGINE. I don't know.

DAVIN. We need to get this thing appraised so we can know what we're up against with this Carlton guy.

REGINE. The lawyer says he wants to offer seventy-five thousand.

DAVIN. I think it's worth much more baby.

REGINE. But it's run down.

DAVIN. Doesn't matter. The land. The space. There is a lot of potential here. He's offering seventy-five to you, what's he offering the neighbors?

REGINE. I didn't get that info yet.

DAVIN. I don't want us to be hasty and give up on fighting for the real value of this place just because that's what this Carlton guy is offering.

REGINE. It's better than nothing, isn't it?

DAVIN. That's what all these kind of folks think. "It's better than nothing." So they can offer people well below the property value of their homes and cheat them of a bigger payment. This is the kind of stuff that's been happening to our folks for generations.

REGINE. Davin, I don't want to go there.

DAVIN. Go where?

REGINE. Into the world of "our people" and "generations." That's your call to action, not mine.

DAVIN. We're doing this now?

REGINE. We're not doing anything. I'm just distinguishing between your need to serve an imagined community and mine to serve the interests that are alive and in front of my face.

DAVIN. Imagined community, Regine?

REGINE. You know what I mean. You seem to have attachments to things just based on the history surrounding it. You seem to think that everyone that looks like you is somehow an extension of you, and I'm just not sold on that idea.

DAVIN. You're completely resistant to the idea.

REGINE. We grew up differently. We know that about each other. It doesn't have to be news right now.

DAVIN. And yet it continues to baffle me how you can sound so elitist sometimes.

REGINE. Don't call me elitist.

DAVIN. I'm calling what I see. You act like the history of our people is insignificant. Why do you have to be so dismissive.

REGINE. I'm not dismissing it but not everybody's history gives them this sense of pride and it's not fair to expect us to. Everybody doesn't want to cling to their past.

DAVIN. I never had a family like you, Regine. I knew one grandmother who raised me like I was her hope for the future. And that's it.

REGINE. Davin, I know this. I didn't just meet you yesterday. We're neck deep in.

DAVIN. I'm just stating the facts. No mother. No siblings that I ever met. No father. Just a grandmother who couldn't afford to leave me the shirt on her back. And here you have a house and treat it like it means nothing.

REGINE. I also had a grandmother who hated my mother for having me at sixteen, and barely spoke a loving word to me. I had a mother who I could never please or satisfy, even when I brought home straight As or got my first promotion at my marketing firm. I had a sister addict who stole from me and lied every chance she could get. That is my amazing legacy. And if I don't want to own it, I don't have to.

DAVIN. You don't have to throw the good out with the bad because you're too stubborn to confront the past.

REGINE. There is no good with the bad. There is not one pleasant memory for me here.

It's my past and if I don't want to confront it, that's my right!

DAVIN. It's not about rights. It's about us. And what's good for you.

REGINE. Davin, don't start doing that. Don't start diminishing me with your psychotherapy talk. I'm not one of your students that you're counseling. I'm capable of deciding what's good for me all by myself.

DAVIN. By yourself?

REGINE. Yes. By myself.

DAVIN. *(Scorn.)* OK. Fine.

> *(Beat. Long tension in the air.)*

> *(Inhale and exhale. They fume silently.)*

> *(***REGINE*** digs in her purse for a snack.)*

REGINE. I'm getting hungry. You?

DAVIN. *(Still fuming.)* Not really.

REGINE. I have some cashews.

DAVIN. So eat 'em.

REGINE. OK. Fine.

> *(***REGINE*** eats cashews. ***DAVIN*** thumbs through a drawer. Finds a letter. Reads something. Laughs aloud.)*

What's so funny?

DAVIN. You a runaway?

REGINE. What? What is that?

DAVIN. A note?

> *(***REGINE*** walks over and looks at the paper.)*

REGINE. Oh shit. I can't believe you found that.

DAVIN. When'd you write this?

REGINE. Musta been five or six, I think.

DAVIN. I didn't know you were a runaway.

REGINE. Attempted runaway. Failed miserably.

DAVIN. Where were you running from?

REGINE. My mother.

DAVIN. To where?

REGINE. The backyard.

DAVIN. Clever.

REGINE. I was five. Not a lot of options.

DAVIN. So what happened?

REGINE. I was at Mother's apartment. Two-family flat with one of her stupid boyfriends. Name was Percy. I hated him. And I hated his name. Always thought she preferred him to me. I thought she preferred everyone to me. She usually left me to my studies and hardly spent any time with me on account of chasing one man to another. I was sick of being ignored, so I gathered a few things. Made a little boloney sandwich with pickles. Had to have pickles. Some chips. My coloring book. No crayons. And my Cabbage Patch doll. Put it all in one of my mother's scarves, and made a proper *knapsack*. Folded this little note, and left it for my mother. Then I ran out into the backyard of the building and hid in the alley good until she came for me. My mother played along. She came into the yard and pretended to give a good search for me. Called my grandmother like she was worried and everything. I didn't realize she could see me from the second floor window. So finally she says loudly to Percy, "I guess I'm gonna have to call the police to go get her. Hope they don't throw her in jail for hating her own mother." I come running out of the alley saying, "Nevermind! I'm back!" She showed it to my grandmother and they laughed at me good. And Granny said she was gonna save the letter for whenever I got any more bright ideas. *(Beat.)* My mother and Percy split eventually and we came to live here. I never knew she still had this.

DAVIN. Good memory?

REGINE. Half good.

*(Pause. **DAVIN***'s phone vibrates.)*

DAVIN. Our appraiser.

REGINE. Ask how close he is. I don't want to be here when the squatters come back. Not without the police.

DAVIN. Says he's got an emergency with another client.

REGINE. What?

DAVIN. He's asking if we can reschedule for later tonight.

REGINE. I don't want to come back here at night.

DAVIN. It's not a bad neighborhood Regine.

REGINE. You can say that knowing someone's toothbrush is upstairs? Knowing someone is living here illegally doing God-knows-what???

DAVIN. It doesn't feel like a drug house. It's kept intact. Someone's made this their home.

REGINE. It's not their home. It's my grandmother's home. God, my personal things are here. I don't even know what else... I mean I'm terrified to think what personal info my grandmother left behind...who knows what they've rummaged through. Who knows what they know about us Davin? I mean, Jesus.

DAVIN. OK, so what should I tell him? The Carlton guy needs an answer on his offer before the end of the week. We need to get it appraised as soon as possible.

REGINE. This is why we should just take the damn money he's offering, send the police over here to toss out these squatters, and go back to our very calm life in Philly. There is nothing left for me here. This place is dead, Davin. And I've got to let it die. That's it.

DAVIN. I'm telling him six o'clock.

REGINE. Davin!

DAVIN. I'll come alone, Regine.

REGINE. I don't want you to come alone. That's not a better solution. "Don't kill me but it's okay to kill my husband."

DAVIN. Regine, nobody's going to kill me.

REGINE. Why do you say things like they're facts without considering that you actually don't know if you're right or not?

DAVIN. Regine.

REGINE. It's not a fact. Your blind faith in a community that doesn't even know you by name is going to kill you one of these days. I love you for your optimism, but you've got to draw the line somewhere. Everybody that looks like you is not on your team.

DAVIN. I didn't say they were. But I'm not going to think the worst of them either. I'm not going to treat this neighborhood in the dark as any more or less scary than any other neighborhood in the dark. You can call it blind optimism. I call it having vision.

REGINE. Even vision gets blurry sometimes. This area is separate from the rest of West Chester for a reason. People from this neighborhood go to parts of West Chester after dark and I guarantee you they will not be welcome. Maybe in the restaurants or places where they spend their money. But let them go wandering around at night. They will be a threat. And the reasons why are complicated. Maybe it's bias. Maybe it's logic. But there is a wall between these communities that has old roots and years of mud on it that we can't just pretend doesn't exist. And one thing I always learned from my grandmother, in spite of her coldness to us, is that you can't erase the dirt that is at the root of a people or a problem. And if you aren't ready to get dirty too, then you don't go diggin' up roots, and you don't go walking into a space blind and altruistic. You just don't.

DAVIN. Baby, you exhaust me sometimes.

REGINE. So do you.

DAVIN. So let's just take a breather from here. Get some rest. And I'll come back this evening by myself. Meet with this appraiser and then we can proceed with selling it to this Carlton guy if that's what you decide. But you didn't just inherit this house alone.

You're my wife. WE inherited this house. And I'm not taking the first offer someone gives me. You understand?

REGINE. What about the squatters?

DAVIN. You want to call the police? We'll send them over here while we're gone. If there's anyone living here, they'll handle it.

REGINE. I don't like this Davin.

DAVIN. Without the actual people here in action, there's nothing the police can do anyway. Who are they going to take to jail? The toothbrush?

REGINE. That's not funny.

DAVIN. Get your coat. We'll send the police over here. And in the meantime, we're gonna take a little tour of your old stomping grounds. You need to fall back in love with this place. Just a little.

REGINE. Why are you doing this? Really. Why?

DAVIN. I... *(The question hits him honestly.)* I'm worried. For you. For us.

> (**REGINE** *grabs her coat.* **DAVIN** *opens the door. As she's heading out:*)

REGINE. Davin I love you. I don't know what you're hoping for. I don't what you think we'll find. And I can't make any promises. But before they bulldoze this place and turn it into a parking lot, I'm gonna find the part of me I lost here, and I'm taking her with me. All of her.

> (**REGINE** *touches his face and goes out of the door.* **DAVIN** *looks around the room and then leaves.*)

> (*The room pulsates with a red glow.*)

Scene Five

(Present day: caution yellow.)

(Dusk settles on the living room of the old house.)

*(**TOSHI** and **TYRIEK** with police tape. They stretch it across the room and over furniture.)*

TOSHI. You got scissors?

TYRIEK. That was my job?

TOSHI. You fuckin' with me?

TYRIEK. You fuckin' with me?

TOSHI. What we 'spose to cut it with? Our teeth?

TYRIEK. You not gonna put this on me. I did more than my share of brilliance on this whole plan.

TOSHI. Without scissors.

TYRIEK. Toshi I swear to God, I'm about to wrap you up in this tape and leave you for the po-pos.

TOSHI. Do it.

TYRIEK. Do. Not. Tempt. Me.

TOSHI. This is stupid anyway.

TYRIEK. You got a better idea?

TOSHI. Believe me, if I did…

TYRIEK. Exactly. You don't.

TOSHI. Like… I understand the deterrent that the police tape is supposed to cause.

TYRIEK. Nobody wants to move into a crime scene.

TOSHI. No, I get that part. That part is kinda obvious.

TYRIEK. So what then. What, for the millionth time, is the part that you are undoubtedly going to question, because you can't just never let my idea rule the day. Because even if my idea is Teflon. Even if it's genius. Even if it's as epic as the Bible, you are going find a flaw.

TOSHI. Cross reference.

TYRIEK. Cross reference?

TOSHI. When the po-pos cannot confirm what real life crime scene *actually* occurred here.

TYRIEK. Do you really think it will get that deep?

TOSHI. Depends on who's snooping.

TYRIEK. If you keep shooting down my ideas, I can guarantee a real life crime scene will absolutely happen here and they will have all the cross referencing they need.

TOSHI. That doesn't make sense –

TYRIEK. I don't care! I'm sick of this.

(**TYRIEK** *tosses the tape.*)

TOSHI. Are you for real right now?

TYRIEK. Very.

TOSHI. You catchin' feelings? Getting an attitude? That's what's happening right now?

TYRIEK. That is what's happening right now.

TOSHI. What, Tyriek, can I do to address your feelings of obvious rejection?

TYRIEK. You can stop being a snob for one.

TOSHI. How am I being a snob?

TYRIEK. Bein' all talented tenth on me. Like I'm part of some brain drain and you are the only one with the actual brain. I did my part. I had my boy rip us off some police tape. I had an idea when you were just swirlin' around with magenta and books on colors and moods and what not, like the answer was gonna come from the spirits of the ancestors or whatever.

TOSHI. Now you wanna insult my spiritual beliefs?

TYRIEK. I'm just sayin', at least my plan was a part of the living world and not relying on the great-grandmothers of yesteryear.

TOSHI. You know what Tyriek, fuck you.

TYRIEK. What kinda shit is that?

TOSHI. I'm sick of your dismissiveness. Like this is a game to me. This is not a game. This is my grandmother's house. This is not some bullshit for someone to just come snatch from us like the gotdamn repossessor oppressors.

TYRIEK. Then tape the damn house up, Toshi. By the time the police come back around for cross reference or whatever, at least these bastards will be scared the hell off.

TOSHI. What time is it?

TYRIEK. What?

TOSHI. What time is it?

TYRIEK. I don't know. My phone is dead. Probably like – what. Almost six.

TOSHI. Didn't Sheldon say those folks asked the police to check the place out by six?

TYRIEK. Yeah. And the cops came by. Found nothin'. Sheldon ripped off some tape from them. They're gone. All is good.

TOSHI. Why would them folks need the place checked by six? What's happening at six?

TYRIEK. I don't know. Sheldon didn't know.

TOSHI. Because Sheldon isn't thorough. I'm thorough.

TYRIEK. Why you gotta insult Sheldon for?

TOSHI. Tyriek those folks is comin' back. At six. That's like now. Or like soon. And we're here.

TYRIEK. Then we gotta finish with this tape. These folks'll see this shit everywhere and think – fuck outta here. This place must be hood. Let's bounce.

TOSHI. Or they call the cops and go – was there a crime scene here? And the cops go – no sir, we're not sure what you mean. And then they go – cuz of all the police tape? And the cops go – what police tape? And then they go – did some stupid pothead loser named Sheldon who is still friends with Tyriek for God-knows-what reasons, rip off your police tape and try to scare us with a fake crime scene? And the cops go – probably. And they go – oh OK thank you. Who cares. We'll take the place.

TYRIEK. That's not how that'll go.

TOSHI. No?

TYRIEK. No. It'll be like – boom. They walk in. Just havin' called the cops. And they see all this tape. And be like – oh shit. The cops must've found some bodies. And they call the cops. And the cops go, crime scene? And they go – cuz of all the police tape? And the cops go – then sir, you should get out of there until we have a chance to follow through with the report. And then paperwork and bla bla bla and real crimes to tackle and no one gives a shit about a report of missing police tape and the people go – I don't trust the cops – cuz nobody should – and then they go, you know what? I can't take this. This place is too hood for me. And they bounce. That's how that'll go.

TOSHI. I don't have time for this.

TYRIEK. It's almost six. Let's just try. And if it don't work –

TOSHI. We'll be arrested.

TYRIEK. We'll move on. Like I said we ought to do in the first place. No harm no foul.

TOSHI. Fuck that, I got a better idea.

TYRIEK. What's that?

TOSHI. We grab those bats in the basement and when the snoopers enter, we start cracking heads.

TYRIEK. I'm pretty sure that's going to end with us in jail and not keeping this house.

TOSHI. Or we find a lawyer.

TYRIEK. Toshi.

TOSHI. Or...we find out who the house is turned over to. Like if my grandmother left it in her own name or my mother's or my...

TYRIEK. Your sister.

TOSHI. It wouldn't be left to her.

TYRIEK. You sure?

TOSHI. Wouldn't make sense. They hated each other.

TYRIEK. All the more reason for her to get it. It's like a... Like a healing thing or whatever.

TOSHI. What you know about healing?

TYRIEK. I know families do that sometimes, Tosh. That's what I know.

TOSHI. It's not her.

TYRIEK. Then you find out who it belongs to and what? You can't just take it.

TOSHI. If I can prove I'm the next successor or something, right?

TYRIEK. Nah...

TOSHI. I can find out how much the owner wants and we can buy it back.

TYRIEK. With what money?

TOSHI. I don't know. But everybody's got a price.

TYRIEK. A price we can't likely afford.

TOSHI. Maybe the price ain't a number. Maybe the price is somethin' else. Like land. Or like, space. Or like power. Everybody's got shit they want. We find out what they want. We stay. They come at six and we greet them, like whassup? And we see what it is. What it really is.

TYRIEK. And if they go – you have five minutes to escape these premises or we call the police.

TOSHI. Then we grab the bats and start crackin' skulls.

TYRIEK. Toshi.

TOSHI. I'm not kidding.

TYRIEK. I thought we were putting the past behind us. We don't do this gangsta shit no more.

TOSHI. Unless it's a last resort. Unless we have no other options.

TYRIEK. Either way we gonna have to flee. If we don't get the first answer you're lookin' for, we gonna have to flee. Just gonna depend on what kinda fugitives you wanna be. Squatters? Drug abusers? Thieves? Or murderers.

TOSHI. We gotta try to scare a muthafucka one way or the other. Streets is the only solution we know, after we've tried everything else.

TYRIEK. Streets is the always the solution after trying everything else.

TOSHI. And there's a reason for that. The street doesn't fail you. The street knows after all the laws and mandates and deeds and writing on the wall, the only true way to balance justice out is to take it down to man to man. Not power and social status and money. Just person to person. Heart to heart. Knuckle to knuckle. And the street doesn't let you cheat or call for backup or call your friend in Washington or whatever. The street is the best courtroom there is.

TYRIEK. Toshi you mean this? Cuz you can't call me to arms just talkin' reckless and sideways. You mean this, I'm goin' into a different mode.

TOSHI. I don't see any other choice.

TYRIEK. If you want me to get violent, I'll get violent. I don't want to. Not really interested in revisiting that lifestyle. But if that's what you want, I'll do it. For you.

TOSHI. You will?

TYRIEK. If not for you, I'd be dead.

TOSHI. If not for you, I'd be high. Right now.

TYRIEK. If not for you, I'd be back in Baltimore on some slow suicide livin'. Stick up man antics or just lyin' in a gutter somewhere. Don't think I don't know that. Don't think for a second I take that for granted, cuz I don't.

I hate your stupid spiritual annoyances and I love 'em too. Cuz they made you better. Cuz they gave both of us some belief that shit ain't always gotta be horrible. I don't take that for granted.

TOSHI. And I don't take you for granted neither. You are good for me. Nobody would ever believe that but I do.

TYRIEK. So I'm sayin', if you want to go to arms, you got to mean it. Because you are the one I will bloody somebody

for. If you feel threatened or unsafe or whatever the
fuck – I got you. Just don't call me to battle lightly. You
got to mean this Toshi. And I will defend this fort like
a warrior.

　　(**TOSHI** *moves to* **TYRIEK**. *She touches his face.*)

TOSHI. Let's take these bitches down.

　　(*Lights shift.*)

Scene Six

(The past: black and white.)

*(**FRANCES** in a historical moment. Hate signs illuminated all around her.)*

("Go home Nigger.")

("Whites and Niggers Eat Together? NEVER!")

("Eat Shit and Die Coon.")

(The signs are accompanied by distant noise and chants. A mob of sorts.)

(A shadow of something flying in the air.)

(A splash sound.)

*(**FRANCES** is dripping in milk.)*

(Lights crossfade.)

(Sepia tone.)

*(**ELSIE** in the mirror. She puts makeup around a battered eye and occasionally touches her belly.)*

ELSIE. *(Into the mirror.)* And when you're born, you will be named Regine Toshi Mae. And if you have a daughter, you will name her Regine. And if you have another daughter, you will name her Toshi. Because that is what we do. My mother was Elsie Frances Mae. And I'm named Elsie. And sister is named Frances. And we keep the names of the women through the line. So you will be named Regine Toshi Mae. And you will be virtuous and educated. You will have a respectable line of work. You will not be your foremothers. You will not sell your flesh or make yourself prey. You will not be tempted by the allure of music and spirits or discarded as a social degenerate. You will have a chance. You will strengthen the line. You will erase the shame of the past. You will not be the memory of whore mothers and bootlegging fathers. You will not be the Jezebel with no village to call home. You will be a mother and a teacher and a wife.

And if for any reason you turn from this path…if you undo this prayer for your survival…you must clip yourself from your daughters. You must detach from them and leave them to a different fate. You must not carry this pain and suffering forward. You must promise me before I birth you, that you will not bring any more suffering into this line. Promise me Regine Toshi Mae. Give me a sign.

> *(A pinch of nausea. She nearly vomits but doesn't.)*

OK. Nevermind the sign.

> *(Lights up on* **FRANCES**, *stepping from black and white into the sepia with* **ELSIE**. *She remains drenched from milk. She holds a broken protest sign in her hand.)*

> *(***ELSIE*** jumps at the sight of her.)*

Goodness Frances!

FRANCES. I oughta threw a brick.

ELSIE. You're a mess!

> *(***ELSIE*** finds a nearby towel. Begins drying* **FRANCES**.*)*

FRANCES. They are hateful. HATEFUL.

ELSIE. I knew this was a bad idea.

FRANCES. This won't stop us none. We'll be back tomorrow.

ELSIE. Tomorrow?

FRANCES. And I'm carryin' my pocket knife.

ELSIE. Frances no, you can't.

> *(***FRANCES*** pushes* **ELSIE** *off of her.)*

FRANCES. Don't you tell me I can't. I can do what I please. I will cut the first livin' bastard that tries me again.

ELSIE. This isn't the way to change! Do you hear me? You
     have to stop this now before you –

FRANCES. I don't care about your inclination for followin'
     broken rules. You gon' stop tellin' me what I can and
     can't do. Group of naysayers wanna sabotage our
     plans. Think them showin' up with signs make us stop
     showin' up with ours? They 'bout the most ignant and
     incorrect sons of bitches that ever tossed a carton of
     milk. Think that's 'spose to scare me? Just makes me
     madder. And they don't wants to see who I be when
     I get madder!

          (ELSIE *gasps. A revealing and uncontrolled*
          welp.)

          (FRANCES *approaches her. Grabs her chin and*
          looks into ELSIE's *face.*)

     What he done to you?

ELSIE. Just leave it be.

FRANCES. He done laid a hand to you.

ELSIE. That isn't the full grasp of it.

FRANCES. He done laid a hand to you cuz of that belly.

ELSIE. I told him everything.

FRANCES. You told him yo' past.

ELSIE. That I'm not high society. That I don't have a mother
     and a father in New York. That I am not enrolled in any
     upper schooling.

FRANCES. You ain't just been hidin'. You been lyin'.

ELSIE. I just needed him to warm himself to me awhile.
     Enjoy some closeness so eventually my history wouldn't
     matter.

FRANCES. But then he got upset.

ELSIE. Furious with me. Says I've made him a fool. Says
     he'll be laughed out of his fraternity. Said he wasted his
     time on a no-count whore.

FRANCES. And after such eloquent talk, you told him you
     were pregnant.

ELSIE. How could I Fran? After he said such things? After he scathed me so? How could I tell him that I was carrying his child?

FRANCES. He gots to know.

ELSIE. Frances, no. Nevermind. It's just wrong. It's all wrong now.

FRANCES. He gots to know cuz it's his duty to provide. Whatever piece of somethin' he earns from that fancy degree, you gots a part of that now. That's fo' yo' child.

ELSIE. This child is marked. For generations. I don't see it any other way.

FRANCES. That child is your blood. Your sin and your salvation. For generations, the Geter daughters will either carry my fight or your frailty. But they ain't gon be cursed. They gon' be cured.

ELSIE. I don't see it any other way.

FRANCES. We got to tell that Edmund who he is. He's the father of your child. And we gon' get us some of that highfalutin legacy money for that child. Gonna be our legacy now. And we gon' bury that legacy here in our home and our land for your children's children. We gon' always be able to keep this land that's ours and build on top of it. And if he don't want to give it up right and proper, then he gon' answer to my pocket knife.

ELSIE. Frances, I can't.

FRANCES. Elsie, I can. This is what we come from. This is what we pass on. Not the pain or the suffering. But the will to survive. Improper upbringing don't got to be our burden or shame. It give us lessons on how to last and we gon' take 'em. You hear me? We gon' take the lesson.

ELSIE. He's staying in school housing.

FRANCES. Then that's where we goin'.

(**FRANCES** *puts her hand on* **ELSIE**'s *chin.*)

I'll fight the White folks. I'll fight the uppity Colored folks. I'll fight anybody tellin' us we ain't fit for more than the gutter. And now you gon' fight too. Like it or not, that's what we got in our blood.

(A flash on **ELSIE** *and* **FRANCES**. *They are immortalized in the dawn of battle.)*

Scene Seven

(Present day: red and magenta splatter.)

(Dim lights on the living room of the old house.)

*(**TYRIEK** and **TOSHI** are shadows. They look out of the living room window like vigilantes. A bat in **TYRIEK***'s hand.)*

*(A key opens the front door. **DAVIN** enters, alone.)*

(He walks in the darkness to a lamp.)

*(Lights up. He sees **TOSHI** and **TYRIEK** staring at him. They are dangerously quiet. They are not their earlier spirited selves. There is a weight and predatorial nature to them that makes this moment very disturbing.)*

(A long pause.)

(Then:)

TYRIEK. You buyin' land nigga?

DAVIN. I...

...

...

No. Not me.

TOSHI. Then why you here?

DAVIN. Just...

...

...

meeting someone. A friend.

TYRIEK. Speak nigga. Why you here? What friend?

DAVIN. Not really a friend. A ...business partner. Getting the place appraised. Supposed to meet him soon.

TYRIEK. Appraised for what?

DAVIN. To sell.

TOSHI. *(To* **TYRIEK.***)* You see that shit? I told you.

TYRIEK. How you figure you doin' the sellin' and you don't own? How you figure that?

DAVIN. It's not me. My –

TOSHI. You do not own this place muthafucka. We own this place.

DAVIN. OK wait a minute. I don't know who you are, but we don't have to be enemies. We don't have to be aggressive or –

TYRIEK. Who says we aggressive?

(**DAVIN** *eyes the bat.*)

DAVIN. Wrong choice of words, maybe. But... I'm not here to cause harm.

TOSHI. You tryin' to kick us out and say that ain't causin' harm? That's what you sayin'?

DAVIN. Nobody's kicking you out.

TOSHI. What are you doin'?

DAVIN. We didn't know you lived here. We didn't know anybody lived here. This place has been empty for five years.

TOSHI. Nope. Wrong. Three months ago this place became occupied. So no vacancies here.

TYRIEK. Who sent you here? What company you with?

DAVIN. No company. Just my wife.

TYRIEK. Liar.

TOSHI. Definitely lyin'. You don't look like you comin' back here to live. You comin' here to stake claim and sell houses you don't own?

DAVIN. We do own.

TOSHI. How you figure that?

DAVIN. Listen, I don't know who you are, but we can talk about this. We can talk. If you put down your weapon.

TOSHI. You don't give the instructions. We give the instructions. You are a guest in our home. It's our rules.

DAVIN. OK.

TYRIEK. When's this appraiser coming here?

DAVIN. Five minutes.

TYRIEK. What's his name?

DAVIN. Does that matter –

TYRIEK. What's his name?

DAVIN. Robert.

TYRIEK. Call Robert and tell him nevermind.

DAVIN. What?

TYRIEK. You heard me.

DAVIN. Listen, before you do something irrational, just hear me out –

TOSHI. Call the man first.

>   (**TYRIEK** *moves in on* **DAVIN** *threateningly.*)
>
>   (**DAVIN** *heeds the caution.*)
>
>   (*Pulls out his cell phone. Dials.*)

DAVIN. No answer. (*Hmph.*) This guy.

TOSHI. Text him.

DAVIN. Just wait a second –

TOSHI. TEXT HIM.

>   (**DAVIN** *obeys.* **TOSHI** *and* **TYRIEK** *look at each other. The room is tense.*)

Give me the phone. Show me the text.

>   (**DAVIN** *shows* **TOSHI** *the phone. It vibrates with a call.* **TOSHI** *reads.*)
>
>   (*A breath.*)

How the fuck – ???

>   (*She looks at* **DAVIN**.)

Regine?

DAVIN. My wife.

TOSHI. You're her husband?

DAVIN. And you???

TOSHI. Her sister.

> *(A moment. **TYRIEK** looks at **TOSHI** for a clue.)*

> *(A long, long pause.)*

> *(Then finally.)*

This muthafucka is family.

> *(**TYRIEK** sets down the bat. Walks over to **DAVIN**. Looks at him squarely.)*

> *(Then suddenly, he grabs **DAVIN** into a chokehold until he collapses.)*

> *(Blackout.)*

End of Act One

ACT II

Scene One

(Present day: red and magenta splatter.)

*(**TOSHI** sits in the lamplight, looking at a document. **TYRIEK** enters.)*

TYRIEK. Alright. We got about five minutes before I gotta wake him. Don't want no serious complications.

TOSHI. Hell no we don't want that.

TYRIEK. I put him in the bed.

TOSHI. Which bed?

TYRIEK. One in the second room. With the quilt and old clothes and what not.

TOSHI. One with all the moth balls everywhere?

TYRIEK. You wanted me to put him in our room?

TOSHI. Granny Elsie's room.

TYRIEK. Oh, now it's Granny Elsie's room? Now we goin' with exact titles and what not?

TOSHI. Always been her room. We just been squattin'.

TYRIEK. Now all of a sudden we just squattin'? What happened to all that ownership? What happened to "This is OUR house Tyriek"? Where'd all that steam go?

TOSHI. She left it to Regine.

TYRIEK. So.

TOSHI. So she chose. It belongs to my sister. There's not shit in here with my name on it.

TYRIEK. Baby you look sad.

TOSHI. This is bullshit.

TYRIEK. I don't like to see you this way.

TOSHI. There was something about not knowing. About the house feelin' like it was left in purgatory or whatever... it made everything feel even and fair. Like the past just squared itself out and we could start over, stake claim and let all the grudges go. And now this. Cold reminder that Regine is still the only one anybody thought was worth a damn. She couldn't leave this shit to me?

TYRIEK. You were a drug addict baby.

TOSHI. Not the point. *(Pause.)* They always loved her more.

TYRIEK. You having sibling envy right now?

TOSHI. She's gonna kick us out.

TYRIEK. You don't know that.

TOSHI. She hates me.

TYRIEK. Maybe not anymore.

TOSHI. I stole her credit cards and ran up $8,000 in debt.

TYRIEK. Easy mistake.

TOSHI. I ruined her credit. That's worse than stealing her car and going to D.C. or taking $500 from her wallet or pawning her locket that Aunt Frances gave her –

TYRIEK. You did all that?

TOSHI. I did all that.

TYRIEK. That was the disease Toshi. You had a disease. That's not your fault. That's like blamin' a cancer patient for losin' their hair or whatever.

TOSHI. That is not the same. That is not even close to the same.

TYRIEK. You changed.

TOSHI. Have I?

TYRIEK. You not the same Toshi. We been through this already.

TOSHI. She won't believe that.

TYRIEK. Then make her.

TOSHI. How?

TYRIEK. Call her. Get her over here.

TOSHI. Maybe text her? Pretend I'm Davin?

TYRIEK. Don't do that.

TOSHI. Why?

TYRIEK. Not a good idea. She'll bring the cops with her. You need her to come alone.

TOSHI. What am I going to say to get her over here alone?

TYRIEK. Tell her it's you.

TOSHI. And when she's like – let me speak to my husband, what am I gonna say????

TYRIEK. You know what to say.

TOSHI. I don't know what to say.

TYRIEK. Street rules. We don't give answers. We get answers. We make the demands.

TOSHI. You want me to threaten her?!?!?!?

TYRIEK. I got dude passed out upstairs. We're already over the line.

TOSHI. Maybe he won't remember what happened. It's not like you hurt him. We just needed some time to think.

TYRIEK. Whether he remembers or not, we're already dirty now Tosh. We gotta do what's necessary. You want her over here? Get her over here. That's the only way this is gettin' settled.

TOSHI. I'm feeling funny again.

TYRIEK. Magenta?

TOSHI. No, red. Strong red energy, Tyriek. What's red mean again?

TYRIEK. I don't know. Like...war? Or somethin' like power?

TOSHI. And also love, right? Red is love.

TYRIEK. Baby. The colors are a distraction. You can't keep hidin' in reds and magentas and not dealin' with the black and grey right here. Time to do what's necessary.

TOSHI. These colors are gonna explode. It's all energy. And I'm feelin' funny like something is not settled in this house.

TYRIEK. So what you gonna do?

TOSHI. I'm gonna call her.

TYRIEK And tell her to come over here, no questions asked. Come alone. And when she says – what about my husband? You say?

TOSHI. He's here. He's fine. But I ain't talkin' about nothin' else on the phone. And if you come here with the cops, it's gonna be trouble. Do not fuck with me.

TYRIEK. That's it. And you hang up.

TOSHI. And I hang up.

TYRIEK. I'ma call Sheldon so he can be on the lookout for cops in case she tries to play us.

TOSHI. She won't. She never has.

TYRIEK. This time may be different. Her husband –

TOSHI. She won't. I know her. She'll be too shook up to change the plan. She's neurotic that way.

TYRIEK. Good.

TOSHI. I don't know how to convince her I've changed after this Tyriek. I don't know how we're gonna get this house.

TYRIEK. You know how we gonna get this house. If fear is the only currency we got, then that's how we pay.

TOSHI. She's my sister.

TYRIEK. So maybe that'll be enough to fix our problems.

TOSHI. This feeling is getting strong. Painful.

TYRIEK. That's just nerves.

TOSHI. No. It's betrayal. Generational betrayal. Eatin' me from the inside and it hurts like a bitch.

> (**TOSHI** *walks over to the window and looks out.*)

Go check on him upstairs. Wake him up and make sure he got water. Make sure he's comfortable. He ain't no hostage. He's family.

> (**TYRIEK** *walks over to* **TOSHI**. *Touches her shoulder. Then turns to head upstairs.*)

*(**TOSHI** takes a deep deep breath.)*

*(The room pulses with red. **TOSHI** feels it in her feet.)*

(She picks up the cell and makes a call.)

No this isn't Davin. It's me. Toshi.

(Lights shift.)

Scene Two

(The past: sepia tone and orange.)

(Sunlight peeks into the room as **ELSIE** *sleeps in the bed and* **FRANCES** *places a cold rag on her forehead.)*

FRANCES. Hey there young'un. How you holdin' up in that belly? Your mama is fast asleep but I see you movin' in there. Stompin' around. You must be leadin' a march of sorts, ain't it? Better not tell your mama though. She'll get to puttin' out that fire quick. Makin' a fuss always scare her so. She believe in a simple, tamed life. But I think you gonna be like your Auntie Frances. Ain't no way to tame us so I can tell you right now you gon' have to convince your mama to let you be. Not be afraid to carve out yo' own space. And you maybe gon' have to fight her. Somebody else'll tell you a child ain't never 'spose to be ornery. 'Specially not to they own mama. But sometimes the young got more vision than the old. Your mama ain't gon' be able to see past her own illusions. She gon' tell you the only way things can be is A-B-C. If you start mixin' up the alphabet and makin' yo' own words, she gon' give you some kinda hell. But even if she do. Even if you grow to see past the sun and she tell you ain't nothin' else up there but sky...even if you see limitless and she limitation, don't forget that she love you. She carry you and sing to you and pray for your safety cuz she love you. And even when that love start to feel like it's choppin' off yo' foot or blindin' yo' sight...remember that love is always a good thing. Whatever you grow to be, you gettin' to be that through her. All the good parts and all the mistakes too. That's what we got from our mama and daddy. That's what we got from our grands. And that's what you gon' get. But if you can...you do your best to take more good than bad. By the time we get down the line, maybe the good'll outweigh the bad so much it won't hardly count none.

(**ELSIE** *coughs.* **FRANCES** *hushes her.* **ELSIE**
wakes.)

ELSIE. Fran? What time is it?

FRANCES. Still early. Don't matter none. You was stirrin'
in your sleep. Nightmares. I just thought I'd cool you
some and chase them haunts away. Don't want 'em
hurtin' the child.

ELSIE. Goodness, was I sweating?

FRANCES. Like a pig at the barbeque.

ELSIE. My back is aching.

FRANCES. Well I can put some ailment on it 'fore I gets to
goin'.

ELSIE. Where you goin' off to?

FRANCES. Down to the Community Center. Plannin' our
"selective patronage" campaign. Time to boycott those
stores downtown next. No hirin' Coloreds? No gettin'
Colored money.

(**ELSIE** *sits up franticly.*)

ELSIE. Another raucous? You're going to cause another
raucous? I thought you were done.

FRANCES. I told you I was done for a spell. While I get to
workin' and makin' us some money at the hospital. But
that work is done now.

ELSIE. Done? What do you mean it's done? Have you been
terminated?

FRANCES. Nobody terminates me. I terminates myself.

ELSIE. Frances what do you mean? Why would you do that?

FRANCES. It's only so many hospital floors you can wipe and
bedpans you can empty 'fore somebody say somethin'
make you throw piss in they face.

ELSIE. Frances! No!

FRANCES. And then I'm gone. But not without my final
earnings. Made sho' I got that first.

ELSIE. You are impossible!

FRANCES. I'm nobody's dirty nigger. That's what the new nurse say to me when I work her shift. "Clean that room, and don't you leave a drop of piss in that pan like you did befo' or I'll have your pay docked for bein' a dirty nigger."

ELSIE. Sticks and stones, Frances.

FRANCES. Piss and bones, Elsie. I waited just 'til she came back in. Made sho' them floors was shinin' good. Made sho' they sparkled. So just when I'm ready to throw that piss in her face, I can admire all my fine works in one quick moment.

ELSIE. You're lucky you're not in the jail.

FRANCES. I didn't wait none for them to fire me. I just watch her gasp and shake. I think she was in pure and unmistaken shock. And I left her there. Walk right past the desk. Grab my pay. And say good riddens.

ELSIE. Every doctor in that hospital...no one is gonna take us now. Do you hear me? No one is gonna help.

FRANCES. You ain't gettin' served by none of them doctors no way. Ain't none of them gonna care 'bout yo' high society ambition Elsie. They ain't takin' no nigger patients. We gon' get you a good Colored doctor like everybody always done.

ELSIE. Edmond told us to get rid of it. He won't help us Fran. None of those Colored doctors are going to go against his family. All that stature. All that prestige. We don't have anything to wage against that. We're defenseless.

FRANCES. I'm gon' tell you one mo' 'gin, just like I told that fool Edmond, when this baby get here we gonna march it right up to his family and demand our cut of the jewels. And if they decide to cross me, we gonna be right outside they house with picket signs and cameras declarin' penance for a bastard child.

You trust me, that ain't nothin' none of them New Coloreds want. They'll buy an automobile and a baby carriage 'fore they give up all that pomp and circumstance.

ELSIE. I feel weak.

FRANCES. You just need to rest.

ELSIE. I don't know what I'm going to do. I don't know how to find a husband or anyone to ever take care of us now that I'm with child. You're it, Fran. You're all I have in the world. I need you to stick around. I don't know how to be like you. I don't know how to fight. I just know how to fill into whatever place I can find. Without a society to belong to where will I be? Or my child? You take pride in our mama whorin' but they ravaged her body, Frances. Do you remember that part?

FRANCES. Don't change who she was to us.

ELSIE. Those klansmen set her on fire and not a negro in town would help to pay for her burial. She had nothing but this home. No community. No one to mourn her when she died. This is what you're telling me to hold onto?

FRANCES. She persevered.

ELSIE. Stop it! Stop coloring it with honor! She was thrown to the wild and swallowed by the night! And I won't let that happen to us, Frances! Do you hear me? You have to tame yourself because I won't be left to die alone! I won't!

> (**ELSIE** *is nearly hysterical.* **FRANCES** *grabs her and hushes her.*)

FRANCES. Shhhhh there. You not alone. Shush that.

> (*A moment of silence.* **FRANCES** *re-wets the rag for* **ELSIE**.)

Nonviolence. That's what the new leadership they got comin' in say. Now me, I don't know how none of it's gonna work. I ain't never been particular to nonviolence in violent times. But if that's what they sayin' we oughta try, then who am I to say it won't work.

> (**FRANCES** *takes the rag to* **ELSIE**'s *head.*)

I know you ain't no fighter. And truth is, this fightin' give me a village I ain't found nowhere else. It where

I belong. And you gon' find exactly where you belong too. It ain't gonna be in no lie. It ain't gonna be in no society that don't welcome you. It's gonna be right here, in this house our Mama earned from her sins. This house gonna always be the bedrock we can return to. You gonna become the community you lookin' for. And I'm gon' be here with you. Nonviolent and tame and helpin' to raise that young'un.

ELSIE. Promise me that Fran? Promise you'll do your work with peace?

FRANCES. Long as don't nobody make me change my mind.

> (**ELSIE** *gives a little laugh.* **FRANCES** *holds her hand. It is a picture frozen in spontaneous hope.*)

Scene Three

(Present day: black and blue.)

*(**TOSHI** sits in the living room in the window. Lights from a car flash across her face. She stands and waits.)*

*(A car door closes. **TOSHI** weirdly fixes her clothing. What the hell for? Who cares.)*

*(Moments later, the front door opens. **REGINE** enters and sees **TOSHI**.)*

(A moment of silence as they stare at each other. It is strange and ghostly. There are generations of women between them.)

(Finally:)

REGINE. Where is Davin.

TOSHI. Upstairs with Tyriek.

REGINE. Who is Tyriek?

TOSHI. My boyfriend.

REGINE. Did you –

TOSHI. He's fine. He's not hurt. They're just giving us some space.

REGINE. Space?

TOSHI. To talk.

REGINE. I don't have anything... I'm not talking to you. I'm getting my husband and I'm getting the hell away from here.

TOSHI. Regine, we need to speak.

REGINE. Do not. Do not say my name like that. Like some innocent baby sister.

TOSHI. I am your baby sister.

REGINE. Not innocent.

TOSHI. Nobody's innocent.

REGINE. I'm going upstairs and I'm getting my husband.

TOSHI. Wait! Don't do that.

REGINE. Don't tell me what to do. You don't get to tell me what to do. You are not the one in control here. I know you think you are. You always think you're ahead of the game or out-conning me. But those days are over.

TOSHI. I'm not trying to con you.

REGINE. I'm done with your threats too.

TOSHI. I'm not threatening you.

REGINE. Really? So telling me to come here without the cops "or else"...that wasn't a threat? Keeping me from speaking to my husband, that's not some kind of threat? Are you crazy?

TOSHI. That's because you won't listen.

REGINE. If your thug of a boyfriend did a thing to my husband –

TOSHI. Don't go up there.

> (**REGINE** *looks at* **TOSHI** *incredulously. But also with fear.*)

REGINE. Or what?

TOSHI. Don't make me do this. Don't make me go street right now.

REGINE. Or what Toshi? You're going to fight me? You're going to have your boyfriend hurt Davin?

TOSHI. I told you nobody hurt anybody. They're upstairs. Talking. Not threats. Not violence.

REGINE. That's bullshit. I know my husband. He'd be down here right now if there wasn't a problem. He'd never leave me here like this.

TOSHI. Fine. We locked him in the old guest room.

REGINE. You did what???

TOSHI. We'll let him out after we talk. Tyriek is watching him. Making sure he's OK.

REGINE. You're going to let him out right fucking now.

> (**REGINE** *walks to the steps.*)

TOSHI. He's got a bat. He'll use it.

(**REGINE** *stops. She turns to look at her sister in horror. And a bit of heartbreak.*)

REGINE. Are you on drugs? Is this…is this another…what do you want? I'll give you all the cash I have but it isn't much, OK? I didn't bring much this time but I'll give you what I have.

(**TOSHI** *stares at her sister sadly.*)

TOSHI. Shit. This is where we're at? Damn.

(**TOSHI** *slowly deflates onto the couch.*)

I know that's my fault. I know you hate me. I know I've done some horrible things.

REGINE. What do you want from me?

TOSHI. I'm not the person I used to be. I want you to see that.

REGINE. Are you living here? Illegally? You've been squatting in Granny Elsie's home?

TOSHI. I've been living here for three months. Me and Tyriek.

REGINE. Oh my God. Oh God.

TOSHI. This is our home.

REGINE. This is not your home.

TOSHI. Always been.

REGINE. Never been. You left this place years ago. Abandoned it and went into the streets. I was left here to deal with Mama and Granny Elsie all by myself. I watched Mama fight for Granny Elsie to make her feel wanted. But all Granny Elsie did was shun Mama for betrayin' the line, 'til it finally sent Mama runnin' off for good. She blamed Mama for every wrong thing you did and when you split, Mama split. And what happened to me? I wasn't enough to stick around for? You had all the love and concern of the women you betrayed and what was I? Insignificant.

TOSHI. You were a success story. The Geter that didn't curse the line. You were the one Granny Elsie hoped for. You were Mama's pride. Top student. College graduate with honors. Followed the rules. Played by the books. You were perfection.

REGINE. That's bullshit.

TOSHI. That's what you were.

REGINE. Bullshit. That's what you convinced yourself I was so you wouldn't feel bad for robbing me blind. For taking my locket of Aunt Frances...the one thing I valued...the one thing I ever inherited from any woman in this family that was actually a treasure...and pawning it for pennies so you could get high.

TOSHI. That was the old Toshi.

(**REGINE** *laughs incredulously.*)

REGINE. And what is this? The new Toshi? The Toshi that squats in other people's homes? The Toshi that steals electricity??? The Toshi that dates thugs with baseball bats and kidnaps peoples' husbands? What exactly is new about this Toshi?

(**TOSHI** *is choked up. Silent. There are no answers here.*)

TOSHI. Nothing.

REGINE. What?

TOSHI. Nothing is new. I'm shit. Always been. Always will be.

REGINE. That's your answer?

TOSHI. You're right. I'm posturin' in this new skin and it's fraudulent. I can't help what's in my core. You were born to be the leader. The one who defies upbringing and society. The talented tenth who's supposed to raise the learning curve for everybody else. But I didn't make that curve. I got bullshit after bullshit diagnosis that somethin' was wrong with me. That I was weak and depressed. And nobody knew what the hell to do about it but try to neutralize me. And oh shit – turns out I can't be neutralized.

REGINE. You can try to make yourself some tragic victim but the truth is you knew exactly what you were doing. You knew who you were hurting every time and you didn't care. And you don't care now. You want what you want. You are incapable of love or consideration. You are completely selfish and self-absorbed and I won't stay here another second and listen to this pity party. Call off your boyfriend with the bat or be prepared to knock me to my death, because I am getting my husband and getting the hell out of here right now.

> (**REGINE** *goes to the stairs again.* **TOSHI** *doesn't stop her.* **REGINE** *disappears upstairs.)*

> (**TOSHI** *sits on the couch quietly in defeat.)*

> (**TYRIEK** *rushes downstairs.)*

TYRIEK. You let her up?

TOSHI. Forget it.

TYRIEK. Am I busting heads or what?

TOSHI. It's over.

TYRIEK. It's over?

TOSHI. I'm not different Tyriek. I haven't changed. I'll never change.

TYRIEK. What are you talking about?

TOSHI. I lied. I'm just a liar. This whole thing is a lie. I'm not over the street. The colors. The healing. The becoming a better self. It's bullshit. It's just another drug. High on pseudo-optimism. And it's gone. The house is hers. She wins.

TYRIEK. Who are you right now?

TOSHI. The real Toshi. The Toshi that is sick and never healing. Never ever healing.

> (**DAVIN** *comes down the stairs, followed by* **REGINE**.*)*

> (*Straight awkwardness.)*

TYRIEK. So um...we evicted?

REGINE. You don't own –

DAVIN. Regine.

(**DAVIN** *silences her. Looks at the others.*)

I should fucking kill you.

(*Silence. They let* **DAVIN** *have that. After all, they did choke him.*)

My wife and I have talked. If you vacate the premises by morning, we won't involve the authorities.

TYRIEK. The authorities.

DAVIN. Only because you're family.

TYRIEK. Where we supposed to go by morning?

DAVIN. That isn't our problem.

(**TYRIEK** *is quiet. Contemplating. He looks at* **TOSHI**. *She is not the fighter he knows right now. She sits defeated.*)

If you make a fuss or try anything else, we're going to make sure they bury you under the jail. Family won't mean a damn thing after tonight.

TYRIEK. You understand we just did what we had to do, right? I mean this wasn't personal. None of this was personal. We just fighting for somewhere to live. Livin' by your wits make you do shit sometimes...but that ain't who we are. That's what we do when we outta options. That ain't who we are.

REGINE. (*Coldly.*) What you do is exactly who you are. Anyone says different is an absolute lie.

(**REGINE** *heads out of the door.* **DAVIN** *follows her.*)

(**TYRIEK** *turns to a broken* **TOSHI**.)

TYRIEK. I thought losin' this place was the thing that you were obsessin' about cuz the place was comfortable. Cuz you felt safe here. But if this was about you lookin' for redemption, I gotta tell you Tosh...that don't live here no more baby. We may have to find that somewhere else.

TOSHI. I'm feelin' strange energy again. Real, real strange energy. What does the color blue mean? Or black? Or black and blue?

TYRIEK. It means we lost, Toshi.

TOSHI. Can you hold me?

> (**TYRIEK** *goes to* **TOSHI.** *Sits beside her. And holds her in his arms.*)
>
> (*She is stoic. The blue from the moon fills the room.*)
>
> (**TOSHI** *drowns in the light.*)

Scene Four

(The past: sepia tone with red splatter.)

*(**ELSIE** holds a new baby. She rocks the baby to sleep. A suitcase is beside her.)*

ELSIE. Regine Toshi Mae, lay your head back down. You've got to get rest before Frances comes home. We have news to tell her and your fussing won't help make it any better. There are things you shouldn't hear. Things that should happen in your slumber so you will be none the wiser. I love your Aunt Frances, I do. But she and I do not see the world the same at all. She wants to disrupt it and I want to live in it. I don't know how we ever became sisters, but we came out how we came out. And she will go on to fight and be an agitator for anything she believes in. But me... I am not her. Women like me must protect ourselves differently than women like her. We have to secure ourselves or we get devoured. That is why when she walks into this room, we will say our goodbyes. We will not be sad. We will not be afraid of her opposition. We will love her and say goodbye and accept our different positions in life. And we will tell her the truth without flinching. That your father has had a change of heart and asked me to marry him. And I have said yes. For you Regine Toshi Mae. For our future. I have said yes.

(A flash!)

*(**FRANCES** is illuminated before a department store. Bright light shines in her face. A **POLICEMAN**'s voice:)*

POLICEMAN. *(Voice over.)* I said move on, nigger. Party's over. Get on outta here right now.

*(**FRANCES** stands firm.)*

(Voice over.) You don't leave in three seconds, we gonna move them feet for you. You and all them other agitators.

(**FRANCES** *stands firm. She folds her arms.*)

One...

(Voice over.) Two...

(**FRANCES** *doesn't flinch.*)

(Voice over.) Goddamn it nigger I said move!

(**FRANCES** *moves as if she's been shoved. In retaliation,* **FRANCES** *spits with rage.*)

(A gasp from a crowd.)

(Then abruptly, the silhouette of a baton comes down on **FRANCES***' head.)*

(Splatters of red blood.)

(She falls.)

(Lights shift.)

Scene Five

(Present day: red love.)

(Lights up on **DAVIN** *and* **REGINE** *in the living room of the old house.)*

(Some things are emptier. Touches of **TOSHI** *and* **TYRIEK** *are missing. Perhaps a shawl removed from the couch. A rug gone.)*

*(**DAVIN** rummages through the drawers.)*

DAVIN. I don't see anything else. They've taken everything out of the drawers.

REGINE. My runaway card?

DAVIN. Wait a minute...

*(**DAVIN** pulls something from the drawer.)*

An old handwritten note, looks like. Don't see your card.

REGINE. Whatever. She can have it. I don't want anything anymore.

DAVIN. The black and white TV though –

REGINE. It's yours baby. We'll take it and sell it to a museum.

DAVIN. Or an antique shop.

REGINE. Wherever you like.

DAVIN. I'll keep this old note too. Might wanna read it later. Keepsake.

*(**DAVIN** stops rummaging and looks at **REGINE**.)*

You OK?

REGINE. I will be.

DAVIN. Baby I told you you didn't have to come back here with me. I could've met Robert and that Carlton guy on my own. It didn't take much to get the place appraised.

REGINE. I wanted to.

DAVIN. You feel better now? We've got the numbers.

REGINE. Two hundred thousand dollars.

DAVIN. I told you we could get more than seventy-five. And two hundred is a steal for a place appraised at one-fifty.

REGINE. That seems unreal for this house.

DAVIN. A lot of homes over here have more value than what's on the surface. That's why you don't let folks shortchange you.

REGINE. So that's it then. We get our money. And Carlton gets a new parking lot for his funeral home.

DAVIN. We can meet him at his office in the morning and tell him we're taking the deal. I just didn't want to give answers in person. He needs time to sweat.

REGINE. You sure that's it?

DAVIN. What do you mean?

REGINE. You don't have an ulterior motive?

DAVIN. Baby?

REGINE. You're not trying to give me time to think? To reconsider? To have some kind of guilt about throwing my sister out?

(**DAVIN** *looks at* **REGINE** *knowingly.*)

DAVIN. Are you?

REGINE. No.

DAVIN. OK.

(*Pause.*)

REGINE. I don't even know why you brought it up.

DAVIN. I didn't, actually –

REGINE. I'm done.

(*Pause.*)

DAVIN. She's not healthy.

REGINE. She's never been.

DAVIN. Both of them. You were right. I was blind and altruistic and maybe that's a problem. Maybe it's my flaw from ignorance. I never had much of a family. I don't know the rules about when to trust and when not to. I just want to believe we can be better. But when I came over here last night... I saw my own...my own family, I guess...and I didn't trust or believe in them. I didn't feel any safety. I just felt like anything could happen to me because no matter how much hope I have for anyone, it doesn't matter if they don't have it for themselves. *(Beat.)* I'm sorry Regine.

REGINE. For what?

DAVIN. I put you in danger, baby. I was blind to stupid, damn near, and that put you in danger. I haven't been able to shake off the feeling that I could've gotten you... or both of us...

REGINE. Shhh...don't do that.

DAVIN. I want to kill that brother.

REGINE. And yet you still call him brother.

    (Pause.)

How do you do that?

DAVIN. Do what?

REGINE. Keep having faith in people even after they give you absolutely no reason to? Even after they break your heart and threaten your life or your sanity? How do you do that?

DAVIN. I don't know baby.

REGINE. You are absolutely beautiful, Davin. You are perfect and wonderful and open with love. Even when the world gives you every reason to be spiteful, you don't take it. And I don't believe for one second that you won't do it again.

That you won't see people who everyone else has given up on and say – maybe they aren't so bad. Because that is who is at your core. And you can't change what's in your core.

DAVIN. It's in your core too.

REGINE. I don't know what's in my core. I haven't known in years. Sometimes I worry that this is as good as I'm gonna get and when you figure that out you're going to disappear.

(A knock at the door.)

*(**DAVIN** rises alertly and goes to stand by the door. He peeks out and turns to **REGINE**.)*

DAVIN. It's her.

REGINE. Fuck.

DAVIN. Want me to let her in? Or call the cops?

REGINE. Is he with her?

DAVIN. Don't see him.

REGINE. OK, Jesus. Let her in. Just let her in.

*(**DAVIN** opens the door cautiously. He squares up, looking for **TYRIEK**.)*

TOSHI. I told him to fall back. I'm alone.

(Beat.)

*(**TOSHI** walks in. **DAVIN** steps onto the porch.)*

DAVIN. I'm going to stand out here and keep watch baby. Let me know if you need me.

(The door closes. Sisters are alone. Quiet.)

*(**TOSHI** sets something on the desk before **REGINE**.)*

REGINE. What's that?

TOSHI. The locket. I got it out of the shop about a week after I put it in. But you had split off to school and... well...

*(**REGINE** doesn't touch the locket. She stares at **TOSHI**.)*

It's not a scam or whatever. It's the real thing.

(Stillness.)

Heard the neighbors on the next porch over talking. They said a guy is coming around here offering people money for their houses. Trying to turn this block into a parking lot. *(Pause.)* You sold it?

REGINE. Selling in the morning.

TOSHI. I guess it's yours to sell.

REGINE. It is.

TOSHI. You remember when we used to play at that tree out back?

REGINE. I'm not doing memories right now.

TOSHI. Right. My bad. That's manipulative and shit. I was just thinking...cuz I don't know if you've been back out there, but those roots is damn near coming into the house. But I guess it don't matter if the house is gonna be bulldozed or whatever. But those roots...they look like they gonna bulldoze this place first anyway.

REGINE. What's your point?

TOSHI. Don't have one really. Just stalling.

REGINE. Stalling for what?

TOSHI. Cuz I don't know how the fuck to say...

...

...

I mean I don't know how you stop your roots from pulling your whole house down, you know? How do you even stop that? They just keep growing and growing until them joints are strong and unbreakable and they will tear down your entire house unless you chop the whole damn tree. That's the only way to stop the spread right?

...

...

...

That's a metaphor. I'm trying to chop the tree, here. Me. Baggage.

REGINE. So chop it.

TOSHI. It's not...just isn't that easy.

REGINE. Granny Elsie made us pick switches from that tree for our spankings. You remember that?

TOSHI. 'Course I do. Everytime we'd fight, she'd send us out back and make us pick our own switch. Like – which one do you want me to beat you with? That has got to be psychological warfare child abuse.

REGINE. You always tried to pick the skinniest thinnest twig. Like over and over again.

TOSHI. Until I finally caught on that skinnier was actually sharper. My legs looked like they'd been turned to leather.

REGINE. That was definitely child abuse.

TOSHI. Nobody knew that then though, so it doesn't count. But if we could report them shits retroactively...

(A faint laugh between them. Pause.)

I've been reading these books. How colors release energy from the chakras and whatever. Colors have energy. Like healing.

REGINE. Sounds weird.

TOSHI. It's pretty weird.

REGINE. So.

TOSHI. So I've been feeling all this energy here. Like reds and magentas and what not. A smoosh of harmony and war. Blues and blacks. Sadness and power. And I'm like – that's what's buried in these walls. All of who we are and what we haven't been able to fix. I've been sleepin' in it for three months. Digesting it. And finding my way back to somethin' better. Here.

REGINE. I'm selling the place.

TOSHI. I know that. But why? You haven't been here in five years. Why'd you come back just to sell?

REGINE. I'm not the one on trial here.

TOSHI. Not saying you are.

REGINE. You know why I've been absent from this house since Granny Elsie died? I was afraid this place had too much devastation for me to handle. I thought the roof would need repair. The electrics would have to be re-wired. There'd be some mildew.

And I thought it would reek of sadness because I couldn't seem to think on this place without feeling horrible inside. Our grandmother believed in being an upstanding Black woman more than she believed in being kind. She believed so much that we should be aspiring for success and climbing the social ladder that she wouldn't speak to us if we fell short of our potential. That was what she called love. Silence and coldness. But you...she worried over endlessly. Me? I could graduate honors and not crack that woman's exterior. And I never knew why.

TOSHI. Maybe she was ashamed.

REGINE. What?

TOSHI. You were everything she could never be. Our granddaddy jilted her at the altar. All she had to show for anything is this house that's been in our family name since our great-granddaddy was pimpin' or whatever. All that talk she always did about our family bein' of great doctors and educators...where were they? Wasn't none of them claimin' us. Didn't none of them claim our mama. Didn't none of them claim her. Then you go off and prove that you can be from shit and still make somethin' for yourself. Maybe she ain't show it to you cuz she couldn't look you in your eye. I know that feelin'. But that don't mean she wasn't proud of you. That don't mean she ain't love you. And that don't mean deep down inside you wasn't nothin' but her mirror reflection.

REGINE. They always said you were cut from the same cloth as Aunt Frances. Said she was a fighter.

TOSHI. She fought for rights. I just fight for shit.

REGINE. Sound like a thin line.

(*Pause.*)

TOSHI. I'm not the same.

REGINE. You seem a little different.

TOSHI. Tyriek is good for me.

REGINE. I don't know about that.

TOSHI. He protects me.

REGINE. He almost killed my husband.

TOSHI. He almost saved my life.

REGINE. Define it how you want.

TOSHI. Don't sell the house.

REGINE. What?

TOSHI. I can be good here. I can turn my life around. I leave here, I go back to the streets. I need this place as much as you need to leave it.

REGINE. I knew that's what this was.

TOSHI. It's not a scam.

REGINE. You want the money? Want me to turn over the deed to you so you can get high for the next five years?

TOSHI. I don't get high. I don't want money. I want the house.

REGINE. It was left to me.

TOSHI. You wanna move on. This place hurts you? Go. But not me. This place is savin' me. This place has people that never called the cops on me. These old folk over here remember. And their kids, some of 'em gone. Some of 'em gave up those houses.

But we don't have to. I can keep this place alive. Keep it in our family. Drop some of that old baggage and turn it into somethin' new. You gonna hold a grudge on me forever? Or you gonna let me change?

REGINE. Nobody changes that fast.

TOSHI. It's been five years!

REGINE It's been one day.

TOSHI. I've been clean nine months. That's real. Nine months and six days.

REGINE. And yesterday you tried to kill my husband.

TOSHI. You know that's not true. He'd be dead if it was true.

REGINE. Or asphyxiated.

TOSHI. Ain't sayin' it was smart. Or good. Or right. Just the only thing we could think of. Desperate.

REGINE. I can't do this anymore.

TOSHI. Regine.

REGINE. Toshi. I. cannot. do. this. anymore. I'm EXHAUSTED. My insides are fucking gone. You took too much from me. Too much. I'm not that invincible. Nobody is.

> *(A moment.)*

You should go now.

TOSHI. You for real?

REGINE. I am.

TOSHI. You giving up on me? On this family?

REGINE. I didn't do this. You did this. I can't just pretend like all that history doesn't matter. I can't forget like you want me to just because it's convenient for you. It isn't convenient for me. It hurts. It hurt me deeply. And I want to believe you're better. I want you to be better. But I am not going to be the fool for you one more time just to make you feel good. I am not.

TOSHI. It's not a scam –

REGINE. LEAVE!

TOSHI. And go where?

REGINE. *(Coldly.)* I don't give a fuck.

> *(Beat.)*

> *(**TOSHI** chokes on tears. Her heart shatters.)*

> *(It takes a world for her to move to the door, but eventually she does. And walks out.)*

> *(**DAVIN** enters.)*

> *(He walks over to **REGINE** and touches her arm tenderly.)*

I don't think I'll ever have your optimism. You should probably know that right now.

DAVIN. You have more than you know, baby. And I won't ever disappear. I'm not going anywhere. Because you have so much more than you know.

> *(**REGINE** falls into **DAVIN**'s arms and he holds her with the might of the world.)*

> *(The room pulsates with red.)*

Scene Seven

(The past: sepia tone.)

*(**ELSIE** in a wedding dress. In the distance, wedding bells. **ELSIE** stands before us, hopeful.)*

*(Lights illuminate **FRANCES**. A bandage around her head.)*

(She holds an envelope in her hands. She opens it slowly and reads.)

(The sisters are in separate spaces but listening to each other.)

ELSIE. Dearest Sister Frances. I hope this message finds you well. I waited endlessly for you to come home, but when you didn't, I had to concede to writing you this note instead. You see someone is waiting for me and... I couldn't keep him waiting any longer.

> *(**FRANCES** sets the letter down. She begins to remove her bandage and re-wrap herself. She takes a wet rag to her own head.)*

FRANCES. It's Edmond.

ELSIE. I know you won't approve of us getting married, but he has had a change of heart and I believe him. He has said that his family has talked and they've decided that it would be best for Edmond and I to marry. And I am so relieved.

FRANCES. He's gonna jilt you. He ain't gonna follow through. That man is bein' forced by his family to do somethin' he don't wanna. And soon as he figure that out for himself, he's gonna be gone.

ELSIE. I know that you won't believe him, but he says he's been promised a job when he graduates and until then we'll live in campus housing. And we'll be a proper family. And he's even said you and I will be able to visit each other. So as soon as I have an address, I'll surely write you.

FRANCES. You ain't gon' be the same after this. A woman jilted can take a lifetime to recover. But a woman 'shamed of her sum parts may never recover. Gon' take it out on generations after.

ELSIE. It isn't that I'm ashamed of who we are. I just know that there has to be more than what we come from. We've got to have options.

FRANCES. I thought I was dead this last time. I thought they had killed me. I felt that billy club hit what could've been the hope outta me. But it ain't. I found that I'm still here. And I'm guessin' I'm goin' back tomorrow and the day after that too. Somebody's got to fight for us to be treated better than mud. Cuz don't nobody wanna be stuck in the mud forever.

ELSIE. I hope this doesn't disappoint you too much. We are Geters. And we will always be sisters.

FRANCES. But we'll never be the same. You'll always be chasing the world that isn't, and I'll always be fighting the world that is.

ELSIE. I love you, Frances.

FRANCES. I love you Elsie. Even though you disappoint me. Even when you return back to this house scorned and bitter. I'll still love you. Even when I have to leave to continue this fight in the south. Even when I join the movement in other cities. Even when I march across bridges for freedom. Even when one day on one bridge I forget my nonviolence and slap the officer who touched me indecent. Even when I'm finally pushed into the river and drowned. I'll love you Elsie. I'll always love you.

> *(Lights come up on* **TOSHI** *and* **REGINE** *in separate worlds. For the first time, it's as if they are watching their grandmother and great-aunt.)*

And I'll forgive you. For leaving and changing the plan and making a stupid mistake.

ELSIE. We are sisters.

FRANCES. Very, very stupid.

ELSIE. It's all I know to do.

FRANCES. I'll forgive you because true love is forgiveness. At the core of who we is...who we always been...is love and fight and togetherness.

ELSIE. Goodbye for now Frances.

FRANCES. Goodbye for now Elsie.

ELSIE & FRANCES. Sisters forever.

> *(A flash immortalizes* **ELSIE** *in her wedding dress.)*

> *(***FRANCES*** *bandaged and ready for protest.)*

> *(They disappear.)*

> *(***TOSHI*** *and* **REGINE** *see each other for a moment.* **REGINE** *holds a letter in her hands. Looks at it.)*

> *(Lights crossfade.)*

> *(Present day.)*

> *(***TOSHI*** *stands in the living room of the old house.)*

> *(***TYRIEK*** *comes in from outside. Brings in a "for sale" sign.)*

TYRIEK. Off the market.

TOSHI. No funeral parlor. Too much life over here for that. We the rebirth.

TYRIEK. Ya'll work out a timeline? Gonna be hard to pay off half of this before like ten years. That's ten Gs a year. That's fair right? You told her that?

TOSHI. We'll talk about it. Baby steps, baby. Baby steps.

TYRIEK. We home owners. Legit.

TOSHI. Half home owners. They still own the other half. Don't get that twisted.

TYRIEK. But no visits right? No unannounced visits right?

TOSHI. We ain't draw up no list of rules. Now all of a sudden you got a house you got rules. Beggars bein' choosers.

TYRIEK. We ain't no beggars. We gonna pay for our half. 100 Gs makes us part owners. Ain't gonna be no beggars.

TOSHI. We got a home.

TYRIEK. We got a home. *(Pause.)* How'd you pull this off again?

TOSHI. I don't know.

TYRIEK. Had a change of heart?

TOSHI. We're sisters.

TYRIEK. What's that mean?

TOSHI. Guess it means I can change. Guess maybe I really am a different Toshi.

TYRIEK. Different choices. Same soul. Don't never lose that soul. I love that soul.

TOSHI. You corny.

TYRIEK. You sexy.

TOSHI. Let's bless every room in our new home.

TYRIEK. Word.

      *(**TYRIEK** goes over to kiss **TOSHI**.)*

TOSHI. With candles stupid!

TYRIEK. Aw shit.

TOSHI. Gotta sage the space. It's deep ancestral stuff livin' here.

TYRIEK. Here we go. What colors you seein' now?

TOSHI. Whole lot of 'em. Some reds. Some magenta. Some yellow.

TYRIEK. What's it mean?

TOSHI. Change.

TYRIEK. Word.

      *(**TYRIEK** finds a candle. Hands one to **TOSHI**.)*

You ready to bless the house?

(**TOSHI** *grabs* **TYRIEK** *and kisses him passionately.*)

(*The colors in the room go off. Magentas rocket. Reds explode. Yellow from the sun shines through the windows. Engulfs them in its rays.*)

(*Spreads out into the world.*)

End of Play

9 780573 708596